A Word About
Ballet

BRIMAX

Pointe shoes

In a ballet company, each dancer has her own supply of pointe shoes. A dancer wears out about ten pairs of shoes each month!

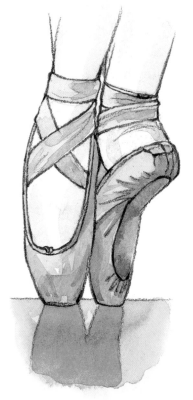

Ballet shoes are made of leather, canvas or satin.

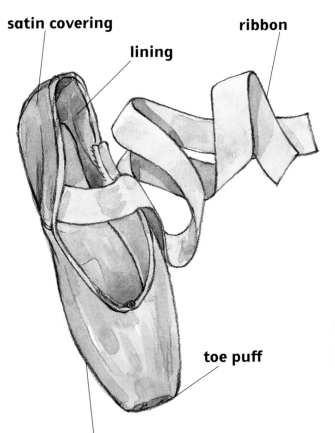

satin covering

lining

ribbon

toe puff

leather sole

En pointe

En pointe is when a ballet dancer stands on the tips of her toes. To do this, a dancer has to be strong enough to lift her body weight off the tips of her toes without straining.

Dancers should only begin going on pointe around the age of 11, when the bones in their toes are no longer soft at the ends.

The toe of a pointe shoe is hardened with layers of satin, paper and coarse material called **burlap**.

Shoe ribbons

As well as being decorative, shoe ribbons hold the ballet shoe on to the foot.

Ballet beginners start out wearing ballet slippers, held on the foot by an elastic or ribbons. They don't use toe shoes (chaussons de points) until their bones are strong enough.

1 Starting with the inside ribbon... the ribbon needs to be taken over the foot and around the ankle to the back.

2 The other ribbon should be crossed over the first one, then taken around the ankle.

3 Both ribbons need to be crossed behind the heel, then brought back around to the front and crossed again, just below the first crossing.

4 Take the ribbons back behind the heel and make a double knot. The ribbon ends should be neatly tucked in under the ribbons.

Costumes

For exercises and to practise their dances, girls usually wear leotards, pink or white tights or socks, and ballet slippers.

leotard

tights

ballet slippers

t-shirt

tights

Boys wear leotards or t-shirts, tights and black or white ballet slippers with elastic instead of ribbons.

tiara

tutu

make-up

tutu

toe shoes

As no words are used in ballet, costumes, make-up and mime play a very important part in the ballet story.

For a special performance or show, ballet dancers wear full costume. The style of their clothing and make-up depends on the part they are playing.

Hair

A ballerina has to wear her hair pulled away from her face to look neat and to show her features.

bun

scrunchie

plaits

Long hair can also be plaited, held together with ribbons and pinned across the top of the head.

Long hair can be pinned into a bun and held in place with a scrunchie.

alice band

Short hair can be pulled away from the face with an alice band.

ballet bag

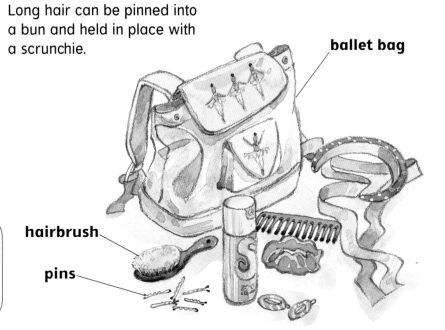

hairbrush

pins

Ballet dancers use large bags to carry their practice clothes and other things to class that they might need.

At the barre

The barre is a wooden rail about waist height, attached to the wall in a dance studio. It is used to give the dancer support while exercising. The different exercises help to warm up the muscles before going on to do dance steps.

pliés

The first exercise is always the plié. Pliés stretch and strengthen the legs.

battement tendue

In battement tendues, the foot slides out along the ground until the toes form a point. This strengthens the legs and feet.

battement frappés

In battements frappés, the ball of the dancer's foot sharply strikes the ground.

French language

Ballet steps were first written down in France, which is why all ballet movements have French names.

grande battements

Grande battements strengthen the legs and improve the height that a dancer's legs can be raised without strain.

posture

A dancer needs to have good posture. Their head and back must be straight and their hips placed directly over the front of their feet.

Steps and dances

Ballerinas and leading men have to learn and perform many difficult and complicated movements or steps in ballet.

corps de ballet

Dancers often join a ballet company to become part of the corps de ballet, or chorus.

pirouette

For this difficult step, the dancer needs perfect balance and strength to spin on one leg.

You can start training to become a professional ballet dancer at sixteen. Training takes at least two years, working and dancing for many hours a day.

arabesque

One of the most basic poses in ballet, where the dancer stands on one leg and stretches the other leg out behind.

pas de deux

This graceful yet difficult movement needs the male dancer to lift and support his partner.

auditions

Trained dancers have to audition to work in a dance company. This means they have to take part in a class as well as perform a solo in front of experts.

Special positions

In ballet, there are five basic positions for the arms and feet. These positions are used at the beginning and end of movement and when passing from one movement to another.

third position
(en troisième)

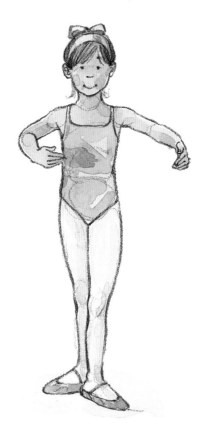

first position
(en première)

second position
(en seconde)

centre practice

After exercising, dancers move to the centre of the room for centre practice, without support of the barre.

fourth position
(en quatrième)

fifth position
(en cinquième)

ports de bras

The way a dancer carries their arms is called ports de bras. Arms should gently curve and fingers should be slightly curved and softly held.

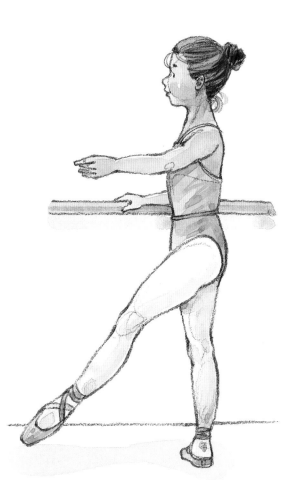

pointing the toes

This is when a dancer's foot is pointed from the ankle with the leg turned out. The foot has to make a straight line with the leg.

Polished performance!

Apart from the dancers themselves, the talents of many other people are needed to put on a successful show.

choreographer

A choreographer decides which steps and movements the dancers will make, then puts them all together to make a finished performance.

stage manager

The stage manager checks that all the scenery and props are safe and in place.

lights

To help create atmosphere on stage, transparent slides of different hues are used to change the shades and tones of a white lamp.

props

Props are specially-made objects, usually much lighter than the 'real thing', and are used by performers on stage.

publicity

Special booklets and posters are printed to tell the public about a show and who will be performing.

backcloth

To make a production look realistic, artists paint life-like scenes on to a backcloth.

Technical crew, stage hands, dressers, special effects technicians, designers – and many other professionals are involved in producing a show.

Glossary

adagio slow and continuous tempo, that involves movements that flow from one to another.

allegro fast tempo, that involves lively steps and jumps.

arabesque a dancer balances on one leg with the other stretched and raised behind.

barre wooden, wall-mounted rail in a dance studio, used by dancers to balance as they perform exercises.

en avant forwards, where the arms are held in front or forwards.

en derrière backwards, the opposite of en avant.

en pointe when a ballet dancer stands on the tips of her toes.

changement a small jump beginning in fifth position with one foot in front, and ending in fifth position with the other foot in front.

corps de ballet a group of dancers who do not dance on their own or in leading roles.

enchainement a series of steps linked together.

finale the end of a ballet.

frappé striking.

grand allegro large jumping steps.

grand jeté a large travelling jump, with legs and arms outstretched.

leotard with or without sleeves, a close-fitting costume worn for ballet classes.

pas de deux a dance for two ballet dancers, usually male and female.

plié the knees bend for this basic ballet movement.

prima ballerina principal female dancer in a ballet company.

solo a dance for one person.

turn-out the way a dancer's leg turns out from the hip socket.

tutu the ballerina's skirt.